EVENTS THAT CHANGED YOUR WORLD

ADA LOVELACE CREATES AN ALGORITHM

by Rachel Werner

PEBBLE
a capstone imprint

Published by Pebble, an imprint of Capstone
1710 Roe Crest Drive, North Mankato, Minnesota 56003
capstonepub.com

Library of Congress Cataloging-in-Publication Data is available on the Library of Congress website.

ISBN: 9780756581183 (hardcover)
ISBN: 9780756581282 (paperback)
ISBN: 9780756581244 (ebook PDF)

Summary: How does a search engine find just the right information? It uses a set of instructions you never see. And that wouldn't be possible without the ideas of Ada Lovelace—the first person to describe an algorithm. Learn about Lovelace's groundbreaking impact on the history of computers.

Editorial Credits
Editor: Ericka Smith; Designer: Terri Poburka; Media Researcher: Svetlana Zhurkin; Production Specialist: Katy LaVigne

Image Credits
Alamy: Science History Images, 10; Associated Press: Frederick News-Post, 21; Dreamstime: Massimo Parisi, 13; Getty Images: AnnaStills, cover (top), Hulton Archive, 28; Library of Congress: 6; The New York Public Library: 4; Newscom: Album/British Library, 14, Everett Collection, 11, World History Archive, 7, 9; Shutterstock: BalanceFormCreative, 25, Gorodenkoff, 24, Jeramey Lende, 23, Prostock-studio, 22; Superstock: age fotostock/Artepics, cover (bottom), 18, Universal Images Group/Pictures from History, 20; U.S. Air Force: Staff Sgt. Christian Sullivan, 27; Wikimedia: 17

Printed and bound in the USA. PO 5853

TABLE OF CONTENTS

Words in **bold** are in the glossary.

A Fascinating Machine

Ada Lovelace is considered the first computer **programmer**. As a young girl, she studied math and science. That was unusual for an English girl in the early 1800s.

Ada Lovelace

As a teenager, Lovelace met Charles Babbage. He was a mathematician and an inventor. He had an idea for a machine. It could complete calculations.

Lovelace was fascinated by Babbage's machine. She began working with him. Eventually, she would create an **algorithm**. It was a set of steps for his machine to use to make calculations.

Lovelace's idea would eventually help make many devices we use today possible.

Did You Know?

Lovelace's mother, Lady Anne Isabella Milbanke Byron, was also interested in mathematics.

So Many Mistakes

In the early 1800s, people did important calculations for tasks like **navigation** and banking by hand. Sometimes they made mistakes.

Charles Babbage

During the Industrial Revolution, people began to experiment with activities machines could do in place of humans. Babbage wanted to create a machine that could do calculations.

Difference Engine

Babbage's first machine was called a Difference Engine. It could complete calculations like adding, subtracting, and multiplying.

Lovelace's interests and social connections helped her earn a spot working with Babbage.

Lovelace came from a wealthy family. That meant she was able to study subjects that interested her, like science and mathematics. As an adult, she read books on her own. At the time, women could not attend college in England.

Lovelace around 1836

Babbage around 1833

Lovelace was also part of important social circles. This helped her meet people with new ideas. In 1833, she met Babbage. He was well known in England.

GLOSSARY

AGILITY (uh-JIL-i-tee)—the power of moving quickly and easily

CHARISMA (kuh-RIZ-muh)—attractive charm or appeal

DRAFT (DRAFT)—process of selecting new players to join a professional sports team

DYNASTY (DIE-nuh-stee)—team or individual that dominates their sport or league for an extended period, often winning multiple championships

LEGACY (LEH-guh-see)—lasting impact and achievements of a person or team

PIVOTAL (PIH-vuh-tuhl)—extremely important, often changing the direction of something

REDSHIRT (RED-shurt)—college athlete who is kept out of competition for one year to develop skills and extend eligibility

ROOKIE (RUH-kee)—first-year player in a professional sports league

SCOUTS (SKOWTZ)—people who search for and identify talent, especially in sports

Lovelace learned about Babbage's Difference Engine. She was impressed. Mechanical objects like that were rare at the time.

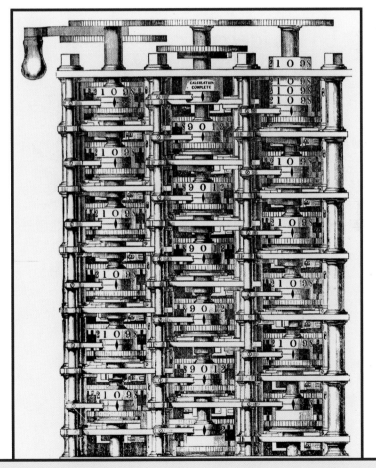

A drawing of part of the Difference Engine

Working Together

Babbage and Lovelace made a great team. Babbage struggled to bring his most complex project to life—the Analytical Engine. Lovelace helped him work on his ideas for the engine.

The Analytical Engine was a steam-powered machine. It would process difficult math problems. It would also be **programmable**. That made it different from other mechanical devices that could do calculations.

Did You Know?

Charles Babbage is considered the "father of the computer."

Analytical Engine

will send down to the Square before tomorrow evening, Brooke's Formulae, & also the _Reports of the Royal Society_ on your machine. I suppose you can get it easily, & I particularly want to see it, before I see you on Wed_dy_ Mor_g_. —

It appears to me that I am working up the Notes with much success; & that even if the book be delayed in its publication, a week or

two, in consequence, it will be worth Mrs Taylor's while to wait. I _will_ have it well & _fully_ done; or not at all.

I want to put in something about Bernoulli Numbers, in one of my Notes, as an example of how an implicit function may be worked out by the engine, without having been worked out by human head & hands first. Give me the necessary data & formulae.

Yours ever
A. A. L

In a letter to Babbage, Lovelace describes calculations the engine might do on its own.

In 1843, Lovelace translated an article about the Analytical Engine from French to English. Her first algorithm was inspired by this work.

Lovelace didn't just translate the article. She added her own thoughts. She added so many notes that the article more than doubled in length!

One of Lovelace's ideas is in a section called "Note G." In it, she explains how Babbage's engine could be used to find Bernoulli numbers. Bernoulli numbers are a series of numbers that are difficult for even advanced mathematicians to figure out. The ideas in "Note G" are now recognized as the first algorithm.

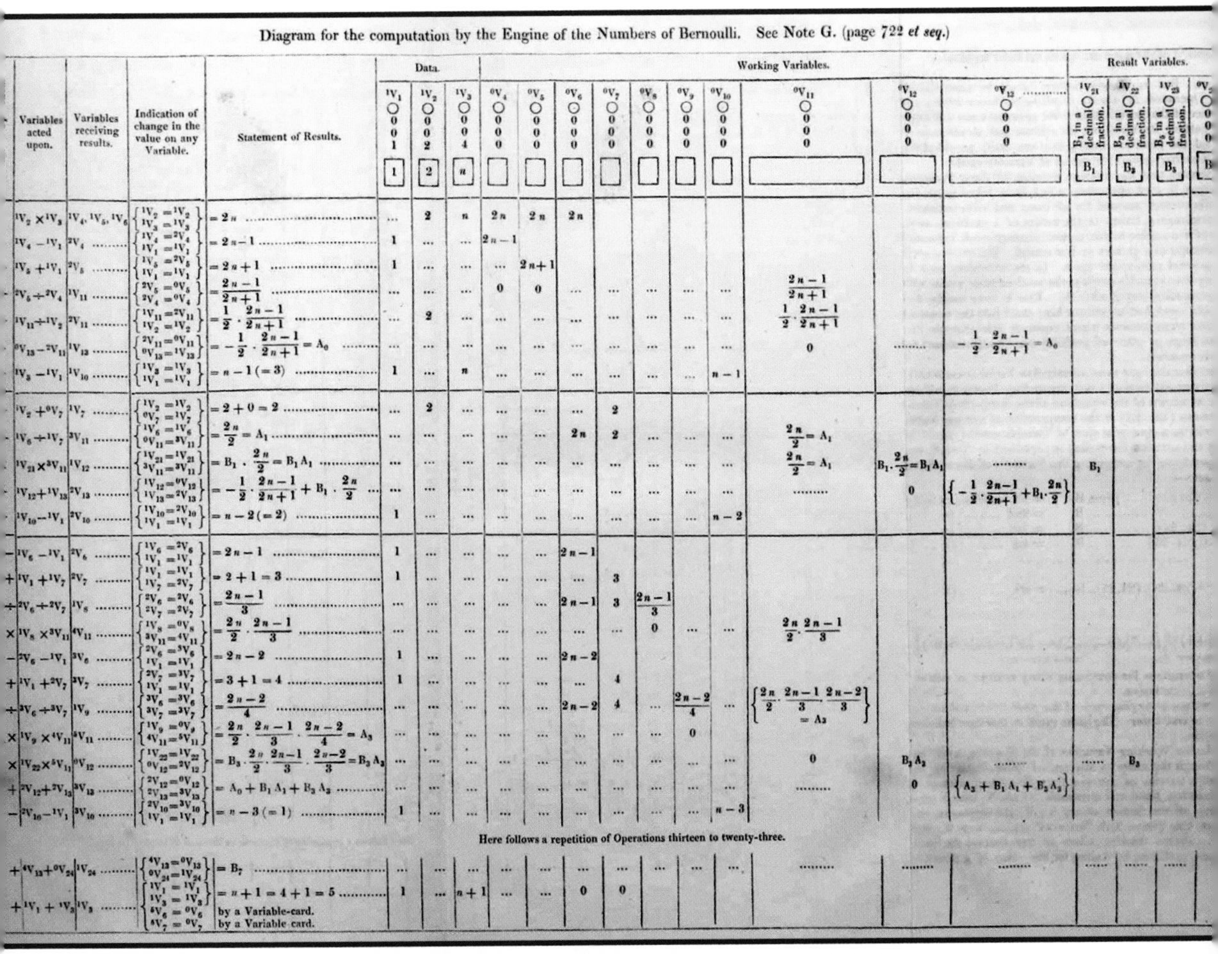

Diagram for the computation by the Engine of the Numbers of Bernoulli. See Note G. (page 722 *et seq.*)

Variables acted upon.	Variables receiving results.	Indication of change in the value on any Variable.	Statement of Results.	Data.			Working Variables.										Result Variables.			
				$^1V_1$ ○ 0 0 0 1 [1]	$^1V_2$ ○ 0 0 0 2 [2]	$^1V_3$ ○ 0 0 0 4 [n]	$^0V_4$ ○ 0 0 0 0	$^0V_5$ ○ 0 0 0 0	$^0V_6$ ○ 0 0 0 0	$^0V_7$ ○ 0 0 0 0	$^0V_8$ ○ 0 0 0 0	$^0V_9$ ○ 0 0 0 0	$^0V_{10}$ ○ 0 0 0 0	$^0V_{11}$ ○ 0 0 0 0	$^0V_{12}$ ○ 0 0 0 0	$^0V_{13}$ ○ 0 0 0 0	$^1V_{21}$ ○ B_1 in a decimal fraction. [B_1]	$^1V_{22}$ ○ B_3 in a decimal fraction. [B_3]	$^1V_{23}$ ○ B_5 in a decimal fraction. [B_5]	$^0V_{24}$ ○ 0 0 0 [B]
$^1V_2 \times {^1V_3}$	$^1V_4, {^1V_5}, {^1V_6}$	$\left\{ {^1V_2} = {^1V_2} \atop {^1V_3} = {^1V_3} \right\}$	$= 2n$	...	2	n	$2n$	$2n$	$2n$											
$^1V_4 - {^1V_1}$	$^2V_4$	$\left\{ {^1V_4} = {^2V_4} \atop {^1V_1} = {^1V_1} \right\}$	$= 2n - 1$	1	...	...	$2n-1$													
$^1V_5 + {^1V_1}$	$^2V_5$	$\left\{ {^1V_5} = {^2V_5} \atop {^1V_1} = {^1V_1} \right\}$	$= 2n + 1$	1	...	...	...	$2n+1$												
$^2V_5 \div {^2V_4}$	$^1V_{11}$	$\left\{ {^2V_5} = {^0V_5} \atop {^2V_4} = {^0V_4} \right\}$	$= \frac{2n-1}{2n+1}$	...	...	...	0	0	...	...	...	...	...	$\frac{2n-1}{2n+1}$						
$^1V_{11} \div {^1V_2}$	$^2V_{11}$	$\left\{ {^1V_{11}} = {^2V_{11}} \atop {^1V_2} = {^1V_2} \right\}$	$= \frac{1}{2} \cdot \frac{2n-1}{2n+1}$	...	2	...	...	...	...	...	...	...	...	$\frac{1}{2} \cdot \frac{2n-1}{2n+1}$						
$^0V_{13} - {^2V_{11}}$	$^1V_{13}$	$\left\{ {^2V_{11}} = {^0V_{11}} \atop {^0V_{13}} = {^1V_{13}} \right\}$	$= -\frac{1}{2} \cdot \frac{2n-1}{2n+1} = A_0$	...	...	...	...	...	...	...	...	...	...	0	....	$-\frac{1}{2} \cdot \frac{2n-1}{2n+1} = A_0$				
$^1V_3 - {^1V_1}$	$^1V_{10}$	$\left\{ {^1V_3} = {^1V_3} \atop {^1V_1} = {^1V_1} \right\}$	$= n - 1 \, (= 3)$	1	...	n	...	...	...	...	...	...	$n-1$							
$^1V_2 + {^0V_7}$	$^1V_7$	$\left\{ {^1V_2} = {^1V_2} \atop {^0V_7} = {^1V_7} \right\}$	$= 2 + 0 = 2$	...	2	...	...	...	...	2										
$^1V_6 \div {^1V_7}$	$^3V_{11}$	$\left\{ {^1V_6} = {^1V_6} \atop {^0V_{11}} = {^3V_{11}} \right\}$	$= \frac{2n}{2} = A_1$	...	...	...	...	...	$2n$	2	...	...	...	$\frac{2n}{2} = A_1$						
$^1V_{21} \times {^3V_{11}}$	$^1V_{12}$	$\left\{ {^1V_{21}} = {^1V_{21}} \atop {^3V_{11}} = {^3V_{11}} \right\}$	$= B_1 \cdot \frac{2n}{2} = B_1 A_1$	...	...	...	...	...	...	...	...	...	...	$\frac{2n}{2} = A_1$	$B_1 \cdot \frac{2n}{2} = B_1 A_1$	....	B_1			
$^1V_{12} + {^1V_{13}}$	$^2V_{13}$	$\left\{ {^1V_{12}} = {^0V_{12}} \atop {^1V_{13}} = {^2V_{13}} \right\}$	$= -\frac{1}{2} \cdot \frac{2n-1}{2n+1} + B_1 \cdot \frac{2n}{2}$ ...	...	...	...	...	...	...	...	...	...	...	....	0	$\left\{ -\frac{1}{2} \cdot \frac{2n-1}{2n+1} + B_1 \cdot \frac{2n}{2} \right\}$				
$^1V_{10} - {^1V_1}$	$^2V_{10}$	$\left\{ {^1V_{10}} = {^2V_{10}} \atop {^1V_1} = {^1V_1} \right\}$	$= n - 2 \, (= 2)$	1	...	...	...	...	...	...	...	...	$n-2$							
$-\ {^1V_6} - {^1V_1}$	$^2V_6$	$\left\{ {^1V_6} = {^2V_6} \atop {^1V_1} = {^1V_1} \right\}$	$= 2n - 1$	1	...	...	...	...	$2n-1$											
$+\ {^1V_1} + {^1V_7}$	$^2V_7$	$\left\{ {^1V_1} = {^1V_1} \atop {^1V_7} = {^2V_7} \right\}$	$= 2 + 1 = 3$	1	...	...	...	...	...	3										
$\div\ {^2V_6} \div {^2V_7}$	$^1V_8$	$\left\{ {^2V_6} = {^2V_6} \atop {^2V_7} = {^2V_7} \right\}$	$= \frac{2n-1}{3}$	...	...	...	...	...	$2n-1$	3	$\frac{2n-1}{3}$									
$\times\ {^1V_8} \times {^3V_{11}}$	$^4V_{11}$	$\left\{ {^1V_8} = {^0V_8} \atop {^3V_{11}} = {^4V_{11}} \right\}$	$= \frac{2n}{2} \cdot \frac{2n-1}{3}$	...	...	...	...	...	...	...	0	...	...	$\frac{2n}{2} \cdot \frac{2n-1}{3}$						
$-\ {^2V_6} - {^1V_1}$	$^3V_6$	$\left\{ {^2V_6} = {^3V_6} \atop {^1V_1} = {^1V_1} \right\}$	$= 2n - 2$	1	...	...	...	...	$2n-2$											
$+\ {^1V_1} + {^2V_7}$	$^3V_7$	$\left\{ {^2V_7} = {^3V_7} \atop {^1V_1} = {^1V_1} \right\}$	$= 3 + 1 = 4$	1	...	...	...	...	...	4										
$\div\ {^3V_6} \div {^3V_7}$	$^1V_9$	$\left\{ {^3V_6} = {^3V_6} \atop {^3V_7} = {^3V_7} \right\}$	$= \frac{2n-2}{4}$	...	...	...	...	...	$2n-2$	4	...	$\frac{2n-2}{4}$	...	$\left\{ \frac{2n}{2} \cdot \frac{2n-1}{3} \cdot \frac{2n-2}{3} = A_3 \right\}$						
$\times\ {^1V_9} \times {^4V_{11}}$	$^5V_{11}$	$\left\{ {^1V_9} = {^0V_9} \atop {^4V_{11}} = {^5V_{11}} \right\}$	$= \frac{2n}{2} \cdot \frac{2n-1}{3} \cdot \frac{2n-2}{4} = A_3$	...	...	...	...	...	...	...	...	0								
$\times\ {^1V_{22}} \times {^5V_{11}}$	$^0V_{12}$	$\left\{ {^1V_{22}} = {^1V_{22}} \atop {^0V_{12}} = {^2V_{12}} \right\}$	$= B_3 \cdot \frac{2n}{2} \cdot \frac{2n-1}{3} \cdot \frac{2n-2}{3} = B_3 A_3$	...	...	...	...	...	...	...	...	...	...	0	$B_3 A_3$	....	......	B_3		
$+\ {^2V_{12}} + {^2V_{13}}$	$^3V_{13}$	$\left\{ {^2V_{12}} = {^0V_{12}} \atop {^2V_{13}} = {^3V_{13}} \right\}$	$= A_0 + B_1 A_1 + B_3 A_3$	...	...	...	...	...	...	...	...	...	...	....	0	$\left\{ A_3 + B_1 A_1 + B_3 A_3 \right\}$				
$-\ {^2V_{10}} - {^1V_1}$	$^3V_{10}$	$\left\{ {^2V_{10}} = {^3V_{10}} \atop {^1V_1} = {^1V_1} \right\}$	$= n - 3 \, (= 1)$	1	...	...	...	...	...	...	...	...	$n-3$							
Here follows a repetition of Operations thirteen to twenty-three.																				
$+\ {^4V_{13}} + {^0V_{24}}$	$^1V_{24}$	$\left\{ {^4V_{13}} = {^0V_{13}} \atop {^0V_{24}} = {^1V_{24}} \right\}$	$= B_7$	...	...	...	...	...	...	...	...	...	...	....	....	....	......	......	......	
$+\ {^1V_1} + {^1V_3}$	$^1V_3$	$\left\{ {^1V_1} = {^1V_1} \atop {^1V_3} = {^1V_3} \right\}$ $^5V_6 = {^0V_6}$ $^5V_7 = {^0V_7}$	$= n + 1 = 4 + 1 = 5$ .... by a Variable-card. by a Variable card.	1	...	$n+1$	...	...	0	0										

A diagram that was part of Lovelace's "Note G"

Lovelace imagined these instructions would eventually help the Analytical Engine solve different problems. It could do that by changing the pattern of numbers or the types of symbols in the algorithm. She was describing a language for machines—**coding**.

At the time, few people understood Babbage's Analytical Engine. He could not get enough money to create a model of his machine. Most of what Lovelace wrote would not be tested for a long time.

Did You Know?

A working model of the Analytical Engine has never been built.

A World with New Technology

It would take nearly 100 years for someone to invent a machine that could process Lovelace's coding. In 1936,

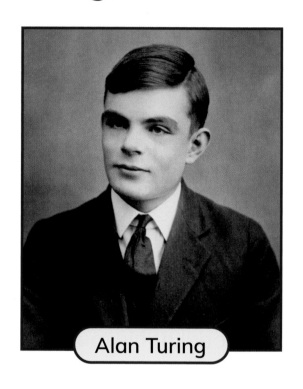

Alan Turing

Alan Turing, another British math whiz, created his Turing machine. It could figure out any math problem.

The first electronic computer built at Iowa State University

The next year, a professor at Iowa State University named John Vincent Atanasoff came up with an idea for a computer that ran on electricity. By 1941, he and a student name Clifford Berry had built the first digital computer in the United States.

Once others understood Lovelace's ideas, new technology became a reality!

A lot of the technology we use today needs programming like Lovelace's algorithm to work. Laptops, cell phones, social media apps, and **artificial intelligence** exist because of Lovelace's ideas.

These tools are programmed to do certain tasks. The coding that people have created to program these tools is proof of what Lovelace believed was possible. Music apps use algorithms to determine which song to play. And search engines need algorithms to help us find information.

Many jobs would not exist today without Babbage's and Lovelace's work. Science, technology, **engineering**, and math (STEM) are all fields that now rely on computers to generate, store, and share information.

Now women are more likely to get college degrees or have jobs in a STEM field. Today in the United States, about 21 percent of students who study engineering are women. And about 19 percent of those studying computer science are women.

Lovelace has received more recognition as an **innovator** too. In 1979, the U.S. Department of Defense began working on a computer language for large engineering programs. They used the language when creating **aerospace** designs and military equipment. It helped ensure the safety of their electronic communication systems. They named it "Ada" after Lovelace.

U.S. military aircraft used Ada programs.

Just as she had imagined,
Lovelace's work has helped open up
a whole new world of technology—
and even more possibilities.

Timeline

1815 Lovelace is born on December 10 to poet Lord George Byron and Lady Anne Isabella Milbanke Byron.

1833 Lovelace meets British inventor and mathematician Charles Babbage.

1838 Lovelace becomes a countess when her husband is made Earl of Lovelace.

1843 Lovelace finishes the article that includes her algorithm in "Note G."

1852 Lovelace dies on November 27. She was 36 years old.

1936 Alan Turing creates his Turing machine.

1941 John Vincent Atanasoff and Clifford Berry create the first digital computer.

1979 The U.S. Department of Defense begins working on a computer language for large engineering programs. They name it "Ada" after Lovelace.

2009 The second Tuesday in October becomes Ada Lovelace Day.

Glossary

aerospace (AYR-oh-spays)—related to making aircraft and spacecraft

algorithm (AL-guh-rih-thum)—a specific set of steps used to figure out a problem or complete a task

artificial intelligence (ar-ti-FISH-uhl in-TEL-uh-junss)—the ability of a machine to think like a person

coding (KOD-ing)—using words, letters, symbols, or numbers to send messages or store information

engineering (en-juh-NEER-ing)—using science to design and build things

innovator (IN-uh-vay-ter)—a person who creates new ideas, devices, or methods

navigation (nav-uh-GAY-shuhn)—following a course point by point to get from one place to another

programmable (proh-GRAM-uh-buhl)—able to follow a set of instructions

programmer (PROH-gram-er)—a person who writes a list of instructions for a computer to follow

Read More

Boone, Mary. *Ada Lovelace: A 4D Book.* North Mankato, MN: Capstone, 2019.

Castaldo, Nancy. *Ada Lovelace.* New York: DK Publishing, 2019.

Rebel Girls. *Ada Lovelace Cracks the Code.* Larkspur, CA: Rebel Girls, 2023.

Internet Sites

Britannica Kids: Ada King, Countess of Lovelace kids.britannica.com/kids/article/Ada-King-countess-of-Lovelace/625448

Computer History Museum: Ada Lovelace computerhistory.org/babbage/adalovelace

National Geographic Kids: Ada Lovelace kids.nationalgeographic.com/history/article/ada-lovelace

Index

About the Author

Rachel Werner is the author of the kidlit *Floods* (Capstone, 2022), *Moving and Grooving to Filmore's Beat* (Capstone, 2023), and *The Glam World Tour* (Capstone, 2025), as well as the nonfiction middle grade title Glow & Grow: A Brown Girl's Positive Body Guide (Free Spirit, 2025). She is on faculty for Hugo House in Seattle, Lighthouse Writers Workshop in Denver, and the Loft Literary Center in Minneapolis, where she leads curricula to educate writers and content producers in marketing their work.